INCOME INEQUALITY
AND THE FIGHT
OVER
WEALTH
DISTRIBUTION

Elliott Smith
Cicely Lewis, Executive Editor

Lerner Publications ◆ Minneapolis

Dear Reader,

I started the Read Woke challenge in response to the needs of my students. I wanted my students to read books that challenged social norms, gave voice to the voiceless, and sought to challenge the status quo. Have you ever felt as if the truth was being hidden from you? Have

Cicely Lewis

you ever felt like adults are not telling you the full story because you are too young? Well, I believe you have a right to know about the issues that are plaguing our society. I believe that you have a right to hear the truth.

I created Read Woke Books because I want you to be knowledgeable and compassionate citizens. You will be the leaders of our society soon, and you need to be equipped with knowledge so that you can treat others with the dignity and respect they deserve. And so you can be treated with that same respect.

As you turn these pages, learn about how history has impacted the things we do today. Hopefully you can be the change that helps to make our world a better place for all.

—Cicely Lewis, Executive Editor

TABLE OF CONTENTS

Megan Rapinoe is cocaptain of the women's national soccer team.

EQUAL PLAYING FIELD

THE US WOMEN'S NATIONAL SOCCER TEAM WAS NEARLY UNSTOPPABLE. They dominated the sport for many years. But as they prepared for the 2019 World Cup, a bigger issue was at hand: equality.

Despite their overwhelming success, the players on the women's team were paid less than those on the US men's team. To the women's team players, that seemed unfair. The women's team is much more successful than the men's team. The men have never finished higher than third place at the World Cup, and that was back in 1930. The women had won three World Cup titles.

In March 2019, a few months before the World Cup, the team took a stand. All twenty-eight members filed a lawsuit against the United States Soccer Federation for gender discrimination. The lawsuit said that women earned $15,000 for making the national team, but men earned $68,750 for the same achievement. Similar inequalities are present outside the US too. For example, the men's World Cup paid $400 million in prize money, while the women's World Cup paid out only $30 million.

Rapinoe led the charge in the fight for equal pay for her team.

Even as the lawsuit continued, the US women's soccer team excelled. They captured the 2019 World Cup to become four-time champions. Shouts of "Equal pay!" rose from the stands at the final in France and from crowds at the team's celebration parade in New York City.

> "We won't accept anything less than equal pay."
>
> —Megan Rapinoe, US soccer player

Soccer isn't the only sport where salaries are unequal. Women's basketball, hockey, and tennis players have also fought for better pay. But because the US women's soccer team has performed so much better than the men's, their lawsuit brings attention to how women are paid unfairly in sports.

Signs of economic inequality can be found everywhere, but many are working toward solutions.

CHAPTER 1
FEW VS. MANY

ECONOMIC INEQUALITY IS AN ISSUE THAT AFFECTS EVERYONE IN THE US. Generally, economic inequality means the differences in how money is distributed among individuals or groups. Differences in income, or the amount of money people earn, is one measure of economic inequality. Whether we're rich, poor, or somewhere in between, the lives we lead depend in part on how big these differences are.

People need money to meet their needs and achieve goals such as earning a college degree or raising children. Large gaps in income distribution make it difficult for people to get food, health care, and housing. Paying for college or owning a home become more difficult. Places with major income inequality see increased rates of illness and crime.

The income gap in the US has continued to widen over the past forty years. Since 1979 people in the top 1 percent of earnings have seen their income grow by over 200 percent. The incomes of the remaining 99 percent haven't grown nearly as much.

"I believe this is the defining challenge of our time: Making sure our economy works for every working American."

—Barack Obama, former president

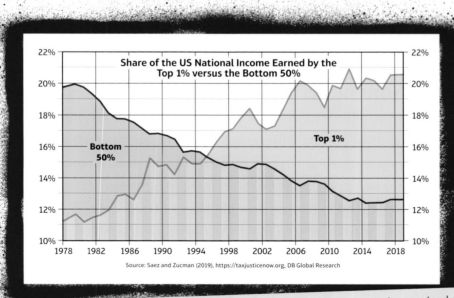

Share of the US National Income Earned by the Top 1% versus the Bottom 50%

Bottom 50%

Top 1%

Source: Saez and Zucman (2019), https://taxjusticenow.org, DB Global Research

This graph shows how the richest people in the US, the 1 percent, have gained more wealth over time, while the bottom 50 percent have less of the share of wealth.

SHARING THE WEALTH

While the US struggles with income inequality, other countries have more equal distributions of wealth. Norway is often considered one of the most equitable countries. Its government provides health care and social services to its citizens. Richer people pay higher taxes to help finance those programs. Because of Norway's greater income equality, it is easier for people to move up the rungs of the economic ladder there than it is in the US.

Norway has universal health coverage, meaning all its citizens have health insurance. In the US, many forego medical treatment because of high costs.

This is a problem because inequality reduces economic growth, meaning there is less wealth to go around and fewer opportunities for people to improve their lives. Rich people grow even richer, while other people can no longer afford the goods and services they want or need. The result is lower participation in the larger economy, which affects everyone, no matter how much money they have.

Some experts describe the effects of income inequality through the metaphor of a ladder, where the rungs represent income levels. If you want to earn more income, you climb the ladder. But in a society with high income inequality, the steps of the ladder become too far apart for someone to reach the next rung.

REFLECT

Why do you think the gap between rich and poor people in the United States has grown so much in the past forty years?

This group of women were part of a movement fighting for women's right to vote in US elections. The gender pay gap shows that a century later, women are still not treated equally to men.

CHAPTER 2
GENDER GAP

THROUGHOUT US HISTORY, WOMEN HAVE MADE LESS MONEY THAN MEN. This difference in income between men and women is called the gender pay gap. While the gap has shrunk over time, it still exists, and not just in sports. When men and women do similar work and have similar qualifications, women earn only ninety-eight cents for every dollar earned by men. The gap is worse when examining the workforce in general. In 2020, women, on average, made eighty-one cents for every dollar men made and annually earn almost $10,000 less than men.

Some states in the US have larger pay gaps than others. In Wyoming, women, on average, make 31 percent less than men. California has the smallest gap at 12 percent. The gap can also be seen in some big cities. In Seattle, for example, women earn about 78 percent of what men do.

The gender pay gap exists for several reasons. Women are often expected to step away from work to raise children or help care for elderly family members. Most of the employees at jobs that pay minimum wage are women. And rarely do women get the opportunity to lead companies. Only 5 percent of CEOs at top companies are women.

"The reality is that if we do nothing, it will take seventy-five years, or for me to be nearly a hundred, before women can expect to be paid the same as men for the same work."

—Emma Watson, actor

The Civil Rights Act of 1964 is supposed to protect women from gender discrimination. But often, employers don't reveal how much they pay each of their employees. This prevents employees from finding out if their employer pays them fairly compared to their coworkers.

The pay gap is even worse for women of color. In 2018, while white women made 79 cents for every dollar that white men earned, Black women made 61 cents, American Indian women earned 58 cents, and Latinas made 53 cents.

Through protesting, lawmaking, and other powerful actions, women have fought back against unfair treatment.

Equal Pay Day in the US was created by a group of women's and civil rights organizations in 1996 to spread awareness about the pay gap between men and women. It is observed in late March or early April. The date changes depending on how far women would have to work into the next year to earn what men made the previous year.

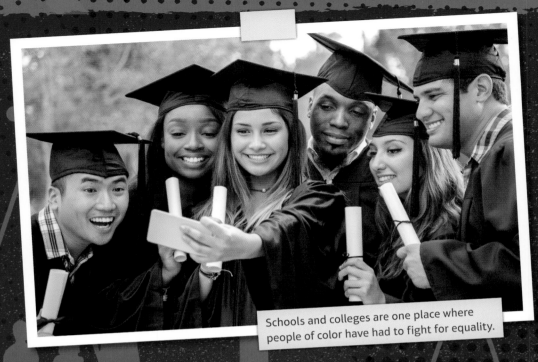

Schools and colleges are one place where people of color have had to fight for equality.

CHAPTER 3
COLOR OF MONEY

FOR BLACK PEOPLE IN THE US, LITTLE PROGRESS HAS BEEN MADE ON INCOME INEQUALITY. In fact, statistics show that the wage gap between Black and white people is the same as it was in 1950. But earnings don't tell the whole story. Wealth, or net worth, is another major indicator of inequality. People can build wealth through owning a home, investing in their educations and careers, earning salary increases, and acquiring other assets. They can also pass on their wealth to their children to create generational wealth.

Wealth is not evenly distributed among racial groups. In 2016 the average net worth of a white family was $171,000, while the average net worth of a Black family was just one-tenth of that. That huge difference means many Black people have a harder time affording big expenses such as homes, college educations, and health care than white people do.

Even in 2020, home ownership for Black people sits at 44 percent, not much higher than it was in the 1960s. And student debt is forcing Black students to drop out of college at a higher rate than white students.

Throughout US history, slavery, racist laws, and discrimination have prevented Black people from building wealth. After slavery was abolished in 1865, many states created Jim Crow laws, which enforced racial segregation and blocked Black people from accessing the same opportunities as white people. While those laws were abolished in 1965, many laws and policies that disadvantage Black people still exist.

The US Commission on Civil Rights works with the government to help to bring equality to all Americans.

ABCs OF MONEY

Money often plays a role in education. In the US, school funding is linked to local property taxes. As a result, schools in more affluent areas often receive more funding than those in poor or rural areas. Parents with more money are also likely to spend it on extra benefits for their kids, such as pre-K classes, summer camps, and after-school tutoring, and they can better afford expensive college tuition. Unequal access to these benefits and well-funded schools is one of the ways income can create educational gaps between two different groups.

Schools in wealthier areas often have better resources, such as updated textbooks and the latest technology. These differences can affect the quality of kids' education.

"It is hard to imagine significantly improving the lives of Black Americans and addressing our long history of racism without a commitment to reduce extreme wealth inequality," Webster University professor Allan MacNeill said.

Racial Income Inequality in the US

White household income is greater than black household income (%):

0 – 9.99%   10 – 19.99%   20 – 29.99%   30 – 39.99%   40 – 49.99%   50% or more

Black household income is greater than white household income (%)

Article/sources:
https://howmuchnet/articles/racial-income-inequality-us
https://howmuchnet/sources/racial-income-inequality-us

Note: Data is from 2018, the latest year available.

This map shows the income differences between white and Black households in each state. White people in the US generally earn higher incomes than Black people.

"We can't declare ourselves the wealthiest nation in the world and still have these major inequities and disparities that are glaringly based on race."

—Monica Lewis-Patrick, president of the community organization We the People of Detroit

Experts are exploring ways to close the wealth gap between white and Black people. One proposed solution is to issue bonds to Black babies at birth. The bonds would be funded by the government and grow over time. Then, as adults, the recipients could use the bonds to pay for college or to start businesses. Another idea is for the government to pay reparations to Black people. These payments could offset the long-term negative effects of slavery and Jim Crow laws, which have limited the generational wealth of many Black families.

The thousands of Occupy Wall Street protesters believed that it was unfair for richer people to have more control over the government.

CHAPTER 4
CLOSING THE GAP

ONE OF THE BIGGEST PROTESTS AGAINST INCOME INEQUALITY WAS THE 2011 OCCUPY WALL STREET MOVEMENT. The protests took aim at the extremely wealthy, many of whom were involved in banking and finance in New York City. The movement spread to several cities in the US. Since then, income inequality has become a key issue in broader protests for social justice and fairness, including the Black Lives Matter and #MeToo movements. Activists for these causes recognize that economic inequality is connected to racism and sexism.

Around the world, people have begun to act against income inequality. In Chile a small protest over a rise in subway fares in 2019 led to monthslong action against economic injustice. Beginning in 2018, the yellow vest movement in France organized protests against the high cost of living.

Protesters in Chile succeeded in convincing the government to write a new, fairer constitution.

No quick fix can solve income inequality. In the US, experts continue to study the issue and explore options to close the gap. Some of their studies show that increasing the national minimum wage to $10.10 an hour would lift 4.6 million people out of poverty. Automatically enrolling people in retirement savings plans would provide some assets for people who struggle financially. And increasing taxes on the top 1 percent of earners could help fund numerous programs to aid those in need.

Income Inequality, 2013–2017

Gini Coefficient 2013–2017 Estimate

- 0.5116 – 0.5976
- 0.4816 – 0.5115
- 0.4516 – 0.4815 (National Gini)
- 0.4216 – 0.4515
- 0.3271 – 0.4215

Source: US Census Bureau 2013–2017, American Community Survey

The Gini coefficient is one way to measure income inequality. This map shows how counties in the US score on a scale from 0 (total equality) to 1 (total inequality).

The Living Wage by US State, 2020

WA $51K
MT $47K
ND $47K
MI $49K
VT $48K
ME $51K
OR $52K
ID $46K
MN $52K
NH $55K
MA $60K
NY $59K
WY $48K
SD $45K
WI $51K
RI $53K
CT $60K
NV $53K
NE $48K
IA $49K
PA $50K
NJ $56K
UT $48K
CO $54K
IL $52K
IN $47K
OH $46K
DE $53K
MD $58K
CA $57K
KS $48K
MO $46K
WV $45K
VA $54K
KY $43K
AZ $51K
NM $48K
OK $47K
AR $45K
TN $47K
NC $50K
SC $47K
MS $46K
AL $46K
GA $48K
TX $48K
LA $48K
AK $54K
FL $52K
HI $61K

Bottom quintile | Second quintile | Third quintile | Fourth quintile | Top quintile

Source: worldpopulationreview.com

> This map shows how much money you would have to earn each year to support yourself and your family in each of the US states. The most expensive states are shaded darker than the less expensive states.

All of these options could help the thirty-four million Americans who live in poverty, along with millions more who struggle to remain above the poverty line. Eliminating income inequality would give more people a chance to provide for themselves, support their families, and fulfill their dreams.

REFLECT

What would you do to help reduce income inequality?

TAKE ACTION

Share with your friends some of the information you learned in this book about income inequality to help spread awareness. You can also try the ideas below:

Donate to groups fighting against income inequality and discrimination.

Research jobs you are interested in to learn about potential gender or racial pay gaps.

Call or email your representatives, and encourage them to help reduce income inequality.

Find out more from organizations that fight against income and wealth inequality.

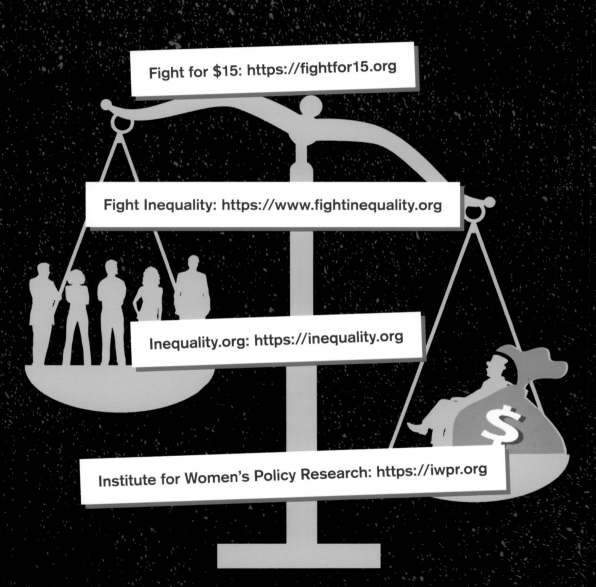

Fight for $15: https://fightfor15.org

Fight Inequality: https://www.fightinequality.org

Inequality.org: https://inequality.org

Institute for Women's Policy Research: https://iwpr.org

TIMELINE

1913: Congress introduces the first modern income tax in the US.

1937–1947: Postwar economic growth leads to a period when income inequality falls dramatically.

1964: Congress passes the Civil Rights Act, which attempts to combat racial and gender discrimination.

1970: President Richard Nixon reduces the corporate tax rate, leading to lower taxes for businesses and higher taxes for middle-class people.

1981: President Ronald Reagan cuts the tax rate for the richest Americans from 70 percent to 50 percent of their income, placing more of the tax burden on the lower and middle classes.

2007: Congress approves increasing the federal minimum wage to $7.25.

2011: The Occupy Wall Street protests begin in New York City.

2013: The Black Lives Matter movement begins in the United States, calling for economic racial justice as part of its mission.

2017: President Donald Trump changes the taxes that corporations pay from a range of 15 to 35 percent to a flat rate of 21 percent. The wealthiest 1 percent of Americans receive 25 percent of the cut's benefits.

2018: The yellow vest protests against tax reforms and high living costs begin in France.

GLOSSARY

affluent: having plenty of money

asset: something someone owns that has monetary value

discrimination: the practice of unfairly treating a person or group differently from other people or groups of people

distribution: the way things are divided or spread out

generational wealth: wealth that is passed from one generation to the next, usually from parents to their children

poverty: not having enough money for basic needs such as food, water, or shelter

poverty line: the US government's official estimate of the minimum income required for basic needs

reparation: the act of making up for a wrong

segregation: the forced separation of a group of people from other groups of people

SOURCE NOTES

6   Mark Osborne and Katie Kindelan, "Megan Rapinoe, Christen Press Speak Out after Ending US Soccer Salary Mediation," *Good Morning America*, August 15, 2019, https://www.goodmorningamerica.com/news/story/us-womens-soccer-team-ends-mediation-equal-salary-64986678.

8   Barack Obama, "President Obama on Inequality (Transcript)," *Politico*, December 4, 2013, https://www.politico.com/story/2013/12/obama-income-inequality-100662.

12   Brittany Bennett, "18 Quotes about Equal Pay from Powerful Women," Bustle, April 1, 2019, https://www.bustle.com/p/18-quotes-from-powerful-women-for-equal-pay-day-2019-17000850.

18   Annie Nova, "These 4 Numbers Show the Dramatic Racial Economic Inequality in the U.S.," CNBC, June 30, 2020, https://www.cnbc.com/2020/06/30/these-4-numbers-show-stark-racial-economic-inequality-in-the-us.html.

19   Paul Wiseman, "Behind Virus and Protests: A Chronic US Economic Racial Gap," AP, June 8, 2020, https://apnews.com/2f549d22162d9d1104c3f402c71e0c44.

READ WOKE READING LIST

Braun, Eric. *Taking Action for Civil and Political Rights*. Minneapolis: Lerner Publications, 2017.

Britannica Kids: Economics
https://kids.britannica.com/kids/article/economics/353081

Equal Pay Today
http://www.equalpaytoday.org

Frazer, Coral Celeste. *Economic Inequality: The American Dream under Siege*. Minneapolis: Twenty-First Century Books, 2018.

Inequality.org: Racial Inequality
https://inequality.org/facts/racial-inequality

Kiddle: Income Inequality in the United States
https://kids.kiddle.co/Income_inequality_in_the_United _States

Stanley, Joseph. *What's Income Inequality?* New York: KidHaven, 2019.

INDEX

PHOTO ACKNOWLEDGMENTS

Image credits: Design: Alisara Zilch/Shutterstock.com; Prazis Images/ Shutterstock.com; artist/Shutterstock.com. AP Photo/David Vincent, p. 4; AP Photo/Seth Wenig, p. 5; Eric Buermeyer/Shutterstock.com, p. 7; Laura Westlund/Independent Picture Service, pp. 8, 18, 22, 23; Geber86/Getty Images, p. 9; Library of Congress (LC-DIG-ggbain-21841), p. 11; AP Photo, p. 13; fstop123/iStock/ Getty Images, p. 15; AP Photo/David Zalubowski, p. 16; Jon Feingersh Photography Inc/Getty Images, p. 17; Gerry Boughan/ Shutterstock.com, p. 20; AP Photo/Esteban Felix, p. 21; Everett Collection Historical/Alamy Stock Photo, p. 26; Gerry Boughan/Shutterstock.com, p. 27 (top); AP Photo/Michel Euler, p. 27 (bottom); Cecily Lewis portrait photos by Fernando Decillis.

Cover: Alisara Zilch/Shutterstock.com; Prazis Images/Shutterstock.com; artist/Shutterstock.com.

Content consultant: Joe Soss, Cowles Professor for the Study of Public Service, Hubert H. Humphrey School of Public Affairs, University of Minnesota

Lerner Publications Company
An imprint of Lerner Publishing Group, Inc.
241 First Avenue North
Minneapolis, MN 55401 USA

For reading levels and more information, look up this title at www.lernerbooks.com.

Main body text set in Aptifer Sans LT Pro.
Typeface provided by Linotype AG.

Designer: Viet Chu

Library of Congress Cataloging-in-Publication Data

Names: Smith, Elliott, 1976– author.
Title: Income inequality and the fight over wealth distribution / Elliott Smith.
Description: Minneapolis : Lerner Publications, [2022] | Series: Issues in action
    (Read Woke™ Books) | Includes bibliographical references and index. | Audience:
    Ages: 9–14 | Audience: Grades: 4–6 | Summary: "Throughout American history,
    income inequality has been a huge problem that harms people of color and
    women. This book explores causes of inequality and its lasting effects on entire
    demographics"—Provided by publisher.
Identifiers: LCCN 2020047818 (print) | LCCN 2020047819 (ebook) |
    ISBN 9781728423456 (library binding) | ISBN 9781728431369 (paperback) |
    ISBN 9781728430706 (ebook)
Subjects: LCSH: Income distribution—United States—Juvenile literature. | African
    Americans—Economic conditions—Juvenile literature. | Women—United
    States—Economic conditions—Juvenile literature.
Classification: LCC HC110.I5 S645 2022 (print) | LCC HC110.I5 (ebook) |
    DDC 339.2/20973—dc23

LC record available at https://lccn.loc.gov/2020047818
LC ebook record available at https://lccn.loc.gov/2020047819

Manufactured in the United States of America
1-49183-49314-3/4/2021